Sarah and David Celebrate Purim!

An Introductory Storybook About the Jewish Holiday for Toddlers and Kids

Written by: Anna Blum   Illustrated by: Mariya Shevchenko

2022

Sarah and David are siblings. Sarah is 4 years old and David is 5 years old. They both love to play, laugh, and see animals. David is very much looking forward to Purim. He has a role in a special Purim play!

The month of Adar has come. Sarah and David's family are preparing for the upcoming holiday.
"Mom, what does Purim mean?" Sarah asked.
"Purim is the most joyful Jewish holiday of the year. The word Purim itself is Persian and literally means a lot—a fate. Purim is a Feast of Lots," Mom replied.

"Mom, when will Purim be?" David asked.
"We are celebrating Purim on the 14th of Adar, which will be quite soon," she replied. "Only the Jews in Jerusalem celebrate Purim the day after, that is Adar 15. Their Purim is called Shushan Purim."
"I can't wait," David said.

"I love Purim," David continued. "On that day everyone wears colourful clothes!"
"Please remember, Purim is not just about dressing up," Dad said. "On Purim, we have four obligations to fulfill. These obligations are called mitzvot."
"What are these obligations?" David asked.
"The first one is reading the Megillah, a story of Queen Esther.
The second is giving gifts to friends and neighbours. The third is eating a special meal and the last one is giving support to those who need help."

"Dad, can you tell us the story of Queen Esther?" Sarah asked. "It all started with the story of a courageous and brave woman called Esther," Dad began the story.

A long, long time ago in a town called Shushan, there lived a good man called Mordechai. Mordechai lived with his beautiful niece Esther. They were Jewish, just like you.

In the same town, there was a king called Ahashverosh. After he broke up with his wife he felt very lonely. He decided to have a contest for the new queen. He and his people looked everywhere to find a smart, kind, and beautiful girl.

Eventually, the king decided that the one person he liked most was Esther and married her. The king, Esther, and Mordechai were very happy. However, Esther had a secret—she did not tell the king she was Jewish.

In Shushan, there was also a man who worked for the king. His name was Haman and he was a bad person. He expected everyone to do exactly what he said. He wanted all people to bow down to him and he did not like Jewish people.

One day Haman met Mordechai. Mordechai did not bow down to him. Haman was very angry and he went to the king and said, "There are some people who should not live with us. They have their own God and their own laws. I think you should get rid of them."

The king listened to Haman and agreed, "Yes, make them go away."

The Jewish people were very sad. They liked living in the kingdom and they did not want to go away. Mordechai decided to send a message to his niece, Esther.

“Esther we need your help! That bad Haman wants to get rid of us all! Please talk to the king, tell him you are Jewish, so he can see he did wrong. We need to stop Haman!”

Esther was afraid that the king would get angry, but she knew she had to help the Jewish people. She prayed and fasted to become brave and have an idea of what to do. Then she decided to organise a special dinner and invite the king and Haman to come.

The king was very happy. After he finished eating, he said to Queen Esther, "What can I do for you to say thank you? I can give you everything you want!"

Queen Esther said, “Please help me! Someone wants to get rid of me, my uncle Mordechai, and all our friends”.
“That is terrible!” the king said. He loved Esther and he did not want her to leave. “Who wants to make you go away?”

Esther pointed at Haman and said, “It is him!”

The king was very angry at Haman. He called his guards and said, “Take away Haman and get rid of him instead!”
Then he decided to protect all the Jewish people and reward Mordechai.

After Haman was gone, King Ahashverosh, Queen Esther, Mordechai, and all the people in Shushan were happy. They decided to have a party to celebrate that all Jewish people were saved.

And now, every year in remembrance of this event we celebrate Purim!

“And this is the story we will listen to twice on Purim — in the evening and in the morning. It will be read in a special way and that is what we called the Megillah,” Dad said.
“Now come and find some graggers, we will need them while reading the Megillah. When we hear the name Haman, we will make a lot of noise!”

While looking for graggers David asked, “Dad, will we also dress up this year?”
“Of course, do you have an idea about your costume?” Dad asked.
“I would like to change into a clown costume,” David replied.
“And you, Sarah?” Dad asked.
“I would like to dress up as a queen, just like Queen Esther,” Sarah replied.

Suddenly, the children smelled beautiful smells from the kitchen.

"Mom, what are you doing?" Sarah asked.
"Haman's ears," Mom said.
"Oh, how so, ears?" Sarah said, surprised.
"Don't worry, these are special cookies that we bake on Purim. They are called Hamantaschen, which means Haman's ears," David replied.
"Mom, what else are we going to prepare for Purim?"
"We have a lot of things to cook," Mom said. "Come on, help me make cookies, and then we will start making Kreplach, special dumplings."

The day of Adar 13th, the day before Purim, had come. Sarah and David noticed that their parents did not eat anything that day.

"Mom, Dad, why aren't you having dinner with us?" Sarah and David asked.

"Today we have Purim Eve. Today we fast, so we don't eat from dawn until dusk. We do this in memory of Esther's fasting and praying to God."
"Should we fast too?" David asked.
"No, you are still too little," Mom replied.

“Kids, come on, let’s make a mishloach manot,” Mom said.
“What is it?” Sarah asked.
“It is a special Purim basket with food and drink gifts for our family and friends. Giving these baskets is one of the mitzvot,” Mom said. “This year we can prepare some sweet jars and cookies.”

Purim day had come! The children got up and put on their costumes. Sarah put on a queen dress, David dressed up as a clown. Mom and Dad dressed up as superheroes.

“Kids, don’t forget about your Purim masks!” Mom said.

In the morning the family went to the synagogue to hear the Megillah reading.

First, the reader started with a special blessing. David noticed that the story was written on a big beautiful scroll. The children sat nicely and listened to the reading. There was a great noise as Haman's name was spoken. After the Megillah reading, the reader recited the special blessing.

The first mitzvah had been completed!

After visiting the synagogue the family went to meet their friends to give them mishloach manot—special Purim gift baskets. They had a lot of fun because their friends were dressed up as teddy bears! They exchanged their Purim baskets and thanked each other a lot for the sweet gifts.

“Chag Purim Sameach!” Dad said to their friends.
“Mom, what does it mean?” Sarah asked.
“It is one of Purim greetings and it means Happy Purim,” Mom said.

The second mitzvah had been completed!

"Kids, it is very important to help and share happiness with everybody during Purim," Dad said. "Now, Mom and I are going to help people who had less luck than us. According to Purim mitzvah, each adult should give monetary gifts to at least two poor people."
"Can we go with you?" David asked.
"Of course," Mom said.

The family visited the charity and supported a few people in need.

The third mitzvah had been completed!

In the afternoon, there was a special event for David. He was going to play in one of the school's Purim spiels! His role was to be the king's guard.

"David, are you nervous?" Sarah asked.
"A bit, I hope I don't make a mistake," David said.
"I'm sure everything will be great!" Sarah said.

Sarah was right. The Purim spiels was fantastic. David did great in the play as the king's guard. Everyone got a big round of applause.

After Purim spiels the family went to see Purim festival on the streets. They had a lot of fun. Hundreds of people wore colourful costumes. They laughed, danced, and sang together.

In the evening the whole family came back home and prepared for a special festive dinner called Seudat Purim. The table was beautifully decorated.

“Kids, come and help me light all the candles,” Mom said.

The family gathered around the table and started to pray. Then they started to eat.

"Mmm, it is so delicious!" David said.
"I'm happy you like it," Mom smiled.

"Honey, would you like to drink a glass of wine with me?" Dad asked.
"Yes, thank you, but just a little," Mom answered and said, "Kids, how about singing a song? Let's sing together!"

The family sang their favourite Purim songs, laughed, and had fun together all evening.

The last mitzvah
had been completed!

"I would like to be as brave as Queen Esther," Sarah said.
"Of course, you will!" Dad said. "You should always remember who you are and not be ashamed of yourself. I'm sure you and David will always be as smart and brave as Mordechai and Esther."

Thank you for choosing our book.
We hope you spent a lovely time with it!

If you like our siblings' story we would appreciate it if you can **share your opinion on Amazon.**

If you want to receive
information about new books from series
or you have any suggestions for our future publications please contact us:

es.publishing.amazon@gmail.com

Happy Purim!

Check the coloring book version of the story on Amazon:

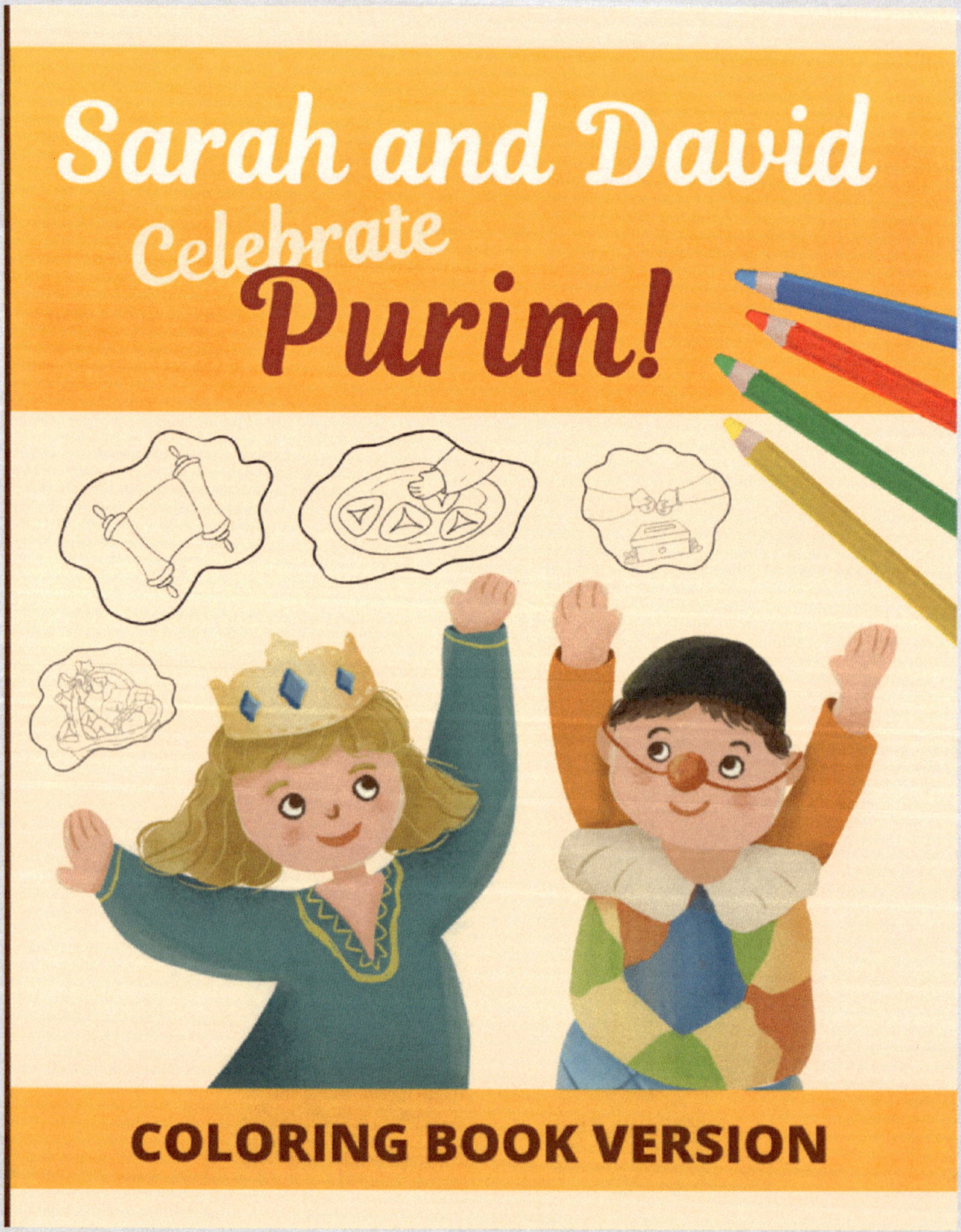

Made in the USA
Monee, IL
27 February 2023

28733329R00019